In the Waiting Room

Farrah Brown

Renew the View LLC.

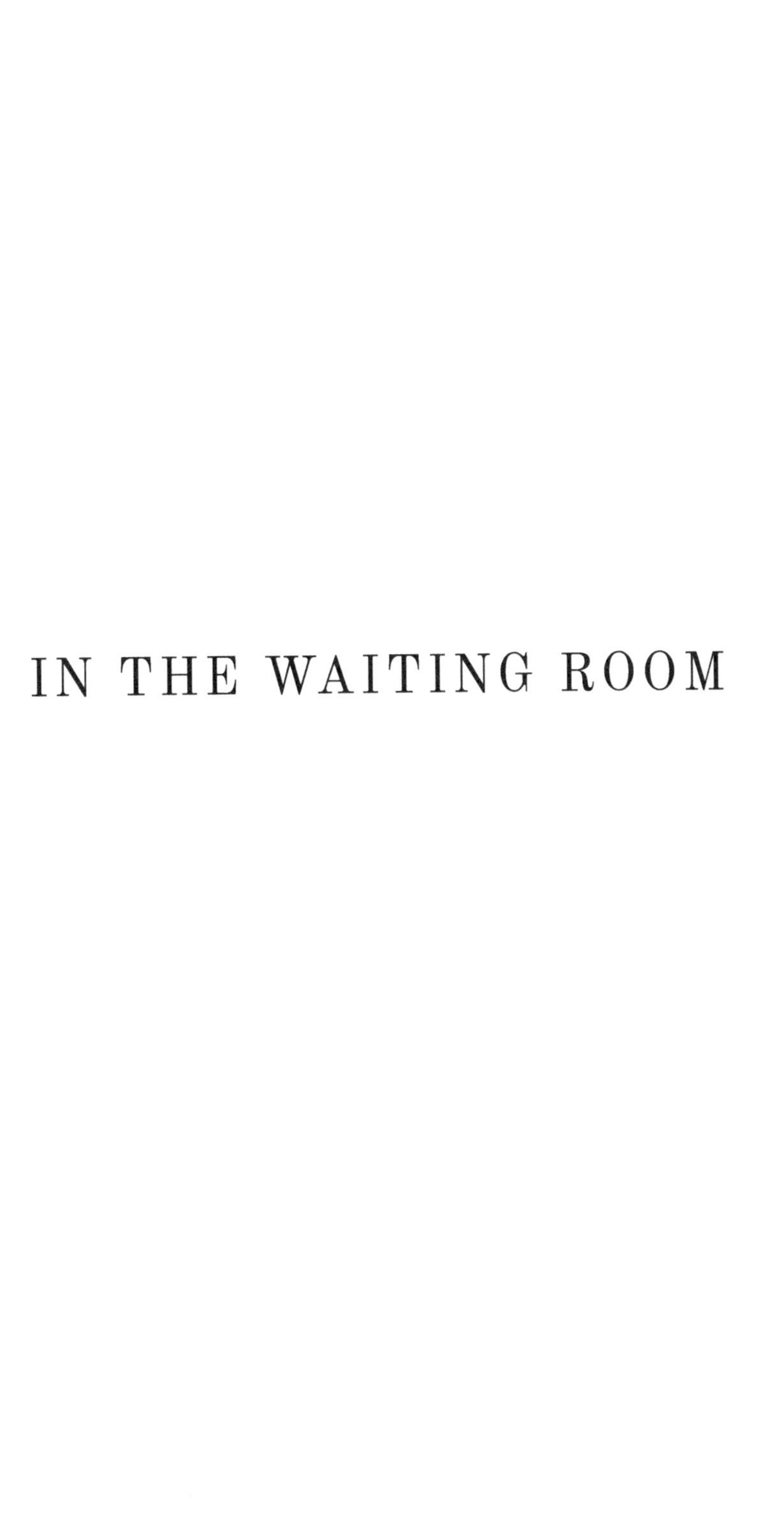

IN THE WAITING ROOM

Romans 12:2

> "Do not conform to the pattern of this world, but be transformed by the renewing of YOUR mind." *(Romans 12:2) NIV*

PERSONAL NOTE:

I was really inspired by this message from the scriptures. It revealed to me so much about what God has in store for us as *His* people. We will face so many trials and obstacles in this life. However, when you set your mind on God, you can get through many things. As the Founder of Renew the View LLC., I am here to encourage you today that changing your mindset can change your life! You can renew your view to reveal the best version of you! Peace and blessings to you.

Farrah-

https://Renewtheview.co

When you think of a waiting room, what comes to mind for you? An initial thought may be a hospital setting. Or the doctor's office? The airport maybe? What about the area designated for candidates during a job interview?

Perhaps the waiting room is a space in your mind designated for processing life circumstances. Moments where we attempt to discern what is happening around us and how to respond accordingly. How you make sense of your life experiences is contingent upon several factors including: 1) the state of your mind 2) the presenting emotions and finally, 3) your focus. Much of my work surrounds the mindset, and here I would like to lean more on the latter – your focus. In the waiting room, God is calling you to focus on *Him*. Your waiting season has a purpose, so let's dive into it today.

<u>SHEILA</u>

A woman named Sheila, has just learned of a building fire near her husband's work site. She just turned on the news and heard the reports. As Sheila's mind began to wander, she frantically started calling her husband's cell phone. There was no answer. Sheila's body began to tense and suddenly she became overwhelmed by the thought of losing her husband.

IS THAT "ANXIETY?"

In those moments, Sheila began to think of the worst-case scenario.

- SHIFT YOUR FOCUS -

When we don't know information,

Don't CATASTROPHIZE, just REALIZE!

<u>In other words, Sheila needs to realize and believe that God does not want us to worry about anything in this life. Instead, He wants us to focus on Him and His goodness.</u>

Talk to God.

This is an opportunity for you. Talk to God. God hears you. He listens to you. He understands you. Set your mind on Him, not your circumstances. Trust that God is working things out for your good in *His* timing.

> "Wait for the Lord; be strong and take heart and wait for the Lord." Psalms 27:14 NIV

Relinquish control. While we cannot control the circumstances before us or those to come, we can be assured that God has our front, our back, and our in-between. Trust and believe that! Hence, there is no need to be anxious!

EXAMINE THE EVIDENCE:

Now, take a few moments to think about how God has showed up in your life. Write those instances down and reflect upon His goodness.

1.

2.

3.

4.

5.

****

It is important to release those thoughts to God first and foremost. We can also release those sensations from our body.

HOW?

<u>TRY SELF-SOOTHING ACTIVITIES:</u>

That is, use your senses to relax and calm yourself when you feel stressed (or anxious). Here are some examples below:

Touch

- grab a piece of ice and hold it
- rub your pet
- squeeze a stress ball
- blow bubbles

Taste

- chew bubble gum
- sip a favorite drink

See

- enjoy the variety of colors through painting/drawing
- step outside to watch nature

Hear

- listen to relaxing music/sounds
- be in silence

Smell

- light a scented candle
- apply your favorite scented lotion to self

<u>JOSEPH</u>

Joseph, a recent graduate from NYU, started working at an architectural firm as a design assistant. After 6 months in the role, the office manager approached Joseph with an opportunity to be promoted to Senior Design Assistant. Joseph was stunned at the offer because he was only in the role for a short period of time. Joseph respectfully declined the offer because he felt that he did not deserve the position. Afterall, he has ADHD, and is what some refer to as a disability. For Joseph, that means that he cannot do a lot of things; in particular, occupy an elevated role due to his disability.

Is that "Imposter's Syndrome" a.k.a. "Self-doubt?"

- SHIFT YOUR FOCUS –

God wants you to understand who you are in *Him.*

Be confident knowing that you are part of His kingdom and remind yourself that,

"I can do all things through Christ which strengtheneth me." *Philippians 4:13 KJV*

God will give you the ABILITY despite your "disability!"

For the believers in the back of the room, let's rephrase this. God can and will use you in your weakness, especially when that is part of *His* plan for your life.

Joseph's inability to see his abilities interfered with the opportunity that God laid before him.

Don't allow self-doubt to rob you of your blessings!

Despite what you may think about yourself, God made you who you are intentionally! He sees what others cannot see in you. How about that!

Here is the key – you must trust and believe that God has a purpose for you and your life, weaknesses at all!

God will qualify the called!

If you can recall, Moses stuttered, and he was a great man of God.

God used Moses.

As evidenced in Moses's life, God can give Joseph what he needs to be successful in the new role, if only he trusts and believes in the power of the Almighty God.

Here's the good news, **God can use you too!**

HERE ARE SOME ADHD STRENGTHS
or (as some call them) "Super-Powers."

1. *Out-of-the-box thinkers*
2. *Creative*
3. *Empathic*
4. *Problem-solvers*

<u>*Let's dive into you for a moment.*</u>

<u>*WHAT ARE **YOUR STRENGTHS**?*</u>

List them below and feel free to elaborate on a separate sheet of paper.

____

____

____

____

____

____

<u>*Mary*</u>

A devoted wife and mother, Mary recently fell ill and could not account for the how, what, or when of her recent health episode. After several days, her husband, Samuel convinced her to get a check-up with her doctor. Mary followed her husband's suggestion and decided to schedule a visit. At the appointment, the doctor performed a battery of tests, including lab work to rule out a few possibilities. "I will notify you in one week," the doctor informed Mary.

Every day during that week, Mary worried her husband endlessly about possible outcomes. "What if it's cancer?" "What if it's life-threatening?!" Mary could not sleep due to the overwhelming thoughts and possibilities.

HELLO WORRY?

Do you worry like Mary? You should know there is another way.

- SHIFT YOUR FOCUS –

While we may have some concerns about our
health and our life in general, Jesus tells us:

"Therefore do not worry about tomorrow, for tomorrow will worry about itself. Each day has enough trouble of its own." Matthew 6:34 NIV

In other words, why worry about something that may not be in your control? Instead, turn your focus to Him and remain hopeful that you will have a good health report.

Give all concerns to God.

Remember, *He* is in control! Not you, your spouse, the doctors, or anyone else – only God!

> "Can any one of you by worrying add a single hour to your life?" *Matthew 6:27 NIV*

Here, Jesus is telling us very plainly that worrying is not beneficial to us. So, why do it? Instead, we can remember the promises that God made to us as *His* children.

Here's a tool to consider,

Try a Gratitude Journal

1. Despite your circumstances, what is 1 thing that you can thank God for today?
2. What made you smile today? This week?

Cultivating gratitude is leaning into a positive mindset. Positive thinking is good for your **mental**, **emotional**, and **spiritual** wellness. Essentially, it is putting your heart in the right posture by not worrying about the situation before you.

Cultivating gratitude primarily involves taking a moment to focus on the good things in your life. While the task is quite simple in nature, it does require intentionality on your part. You can do a little each day, in fact.

Remember, anything is possible with God!

<u>**YOU GOT THIS!**</u>

Available at Amazon!

<u>Rebe</u>

Rebe is what some refer to as a "hopeless romantic." She desires a steady romantic relationship in her life but has not been successful in that department. Over the last 5 years, she has had 4 boyfriends – 2 of whom were fiancées. However, none of those relationships were sustained for one reason or another. What's more, she hates the idea of being single. It has been one year since the breakup between Rebe and Mark, and she is praying to God constantly asking: "why can't I keep a man?"

HELLO LONLINESS?

Sometimes, we are so desperate for something that we don't see the blessings before us. God knows the desires of Rebe's heart, which is to have a long-standing, romantic relationship – even hopes for marriage. In Rebe's case, she was attracted to her ex-fiancée's strong work ethic. Mark devoted so much time to his career and made a pretty substantial income. What Rebe did not realize was Mark lied and cheated his way to the top. Perhaps God was saving her from a man with no character.

> "For I know the plans I have for you," declares the Lord, "plans to prosper you and not to harm you, plans to give you hope and a future." *Jeremiah 29:11 NIV*

Sometimes, God will remove people from our lives to prevent us from falling into darkness. We won't see the inner workings of God's plan but know that He *always* has a purpose for our lives.

If someone is disconnected from your life, take it as a blessing, not a loss. God is concerned about our heart so, while waiting on the right man to come her way, it is important for Rebe to prepare her heart and mind to receive what God has in store for her.

In the waiting season, maybe God is saying to you, focus on Him instead of pursuing a romantic relationship. In due time, in *His* time – if you allow God to move- perhaps it will happen for you.

SHIFT YOUR FOCUS

Reflect on the following:

1. What is your purpose?
2. What has God called you to do with your life?
3. Do you know your gifts?
4. What are you passionate about in life?
5. Have you talked to God about your dreams, aspirations, or goals?

Adam

Adam, an aspiring actor from New York, is married to Harrah, a real estate lawyer. While navigating the legal system day to day, Harrah supports Adam's dream of becoming a full-time actor. Taking auditions during the day is the name of the game for Adam as he manages a hotel at night. Aside from the occasional acting gig, Adam is faced with multiple rejections. "They didn't select me hun," he reveals to his wife after a long day of auditions. "I don't know why I even try."

Not only is Harrah supportive all around, but she carries so much hope in her heart for her husband, Adam. "Adam, don't you worry – your big break will come one day soon! I just know it!"

One evening, the phone rang and with so much anticipation and excitement, Harrah exclaimed,

"Adam this could be it! Your big break!"

With a smug look, Adam turned to his wife and uttered: "Probably not this time hun – I never get the job. It's always a 'sorry,' or a 'not selected for this one Mr. Smith…' I just can't…I'm tired of this. They just don't like me. Maybe I'm just not cut out for this after all."

NEGATIVE THINKING

There are times in our lives when we are disappointed by people and discouraged by circumstances. The good news is that God is there through it all!

SHIFT YOUR FOCUS

Today we can recognize the blessing in rejection.

Perhaps the "no" of the day was God letting you know that a better opportunity is waiting for you. You must trust and believe that!

We can find encouragement in the words of Jesus:

> "Ask and it will be given to you; seek and you will find; knock and the door will be opened to you." *Matthew 7:7 NIV*

While you are waiting for that phone call i.e., that next opportunity, ask God for what you want. Then, hold onto the hope and have faith that He will see it through for you.

How can you experience God's goodness when you are ruminating on the negative?

Dismiss negative thinking.

Negative thinking welcomes sin. How? This type of mindset opens the door for the enemy to feed you lies about who you are, and what God is doing in your life.

So, change your perspective about your rejection!

In Adam's case, he was only able to see negative outcomes instead of holding on to hope like his wife, Harrah. If you trust God, you know that one day, the right opportunity will come your way. It will all change for the better.

God knows your heart's desires. So, in the meantime praise Him. Thank Him. God sees you. He hears you. He understands you. God loves you.

Clear your mind of negative thinking and invite Jesus into your heart today!

As a mindset and wellness coach, I want to remind you that your mind is so powerful! When you experience things in life, how you process that encounter really matters. In other words, your thoughts affect your emotions, and your emotions impact your behaviors. In the end, it is your mindset that determines how you show up in the world!

There is an interconnectedness between what we think, feel, and do after an experience.

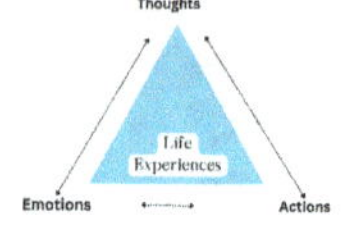

The bottom line is:

Changing your mindset can change your life!

Time for some action!

Here are some exercises to
ENCOURAGE POSITIVE THINKING:

1. **Scenario**: a glass has 50% water in it. Is the glass half full? Or half empty?
2. **Scenario:** At a party, the birthday person has 1 gift on the table in a room full of friends and loved ones. Is there a lack of gifts? Or an appreciation for the 1 gift there?
3. **Scenario**: You texted a friend and did not get a text back. It has been an hour since the initial communication. What are your thoughts there? Do you give grace to your friend or think of the worst-case scenario?

Here, the idea is to focus on what you have, not on the things or people that are not present. In other words, be grateful for those acting gigs that come to fruition Adam! That is the epitome of *positive thinking.*

What you say, especially to yourself, can either uplift or discourage you. So, it is important to only speak life to yourself to remain in a positive mindset.

Remember,

<u>YOUR WORDS MATTER!</u>

And your perspective really matters.

TRY POSITIVE AFFIRMATIONS

Affirmations are words or phrases that highlight who you are or who you aspire to be. Affirmations are positive in nature and are meant to encourage you to think positively about yourself. You can implement them into your daily routine for more impact.

Speak in love to yourself and about yourself; that is what God desires for you. Afterall, you are a child of the Most High!

Examples:

1. *I am blessed and highly favored.*
2. *I am walking into abundance today.*
3. *Today will be a good day.*

TIME FOR SOME ACTION!

WHAT ARE YOUR AFFIRMATIONS TODAY?

____

____

____

____

____

"Name It, Frame It, Challenge"

@Renewtheview

- Choose your favorite positive affirmation of the week.
- Frame that affirmation and place it around your home or office for more encouragement. <u>*(Be intentional* about this!)</u>
- Take a picture of the framed affirmation and post it on Instagram using the following hashtags: **#Renew_theView & #NameItFrameItChallenge**

YOU GOT THIS!

God is always there!

<u>Everette</u>

For the last 8 years, Everette has worked as a software engineer at a major pharmaceutical company in town. For the first 5 years, Everette really enjoyed the work – coming in 1 hour early each day to support the departmental needs. On occasion, he would even volunteer his time on Saturdays to show himself as the ultimate team player. By year 7, Everette found himself working 6 days out of the week, every single week. He was so loyal to the company that he never once thought about how exhausted he was both physically and mentally. His friends noticed how he no longer wanted to hang out - as the group would get together every other week. Every task started to feel like too much. He began to lose focus on those projects he once navigated with ease. Everette started to dread the job that he once enjoyed. On one summer evening, Everette decided that he could not go into work the next day. Day 2, he could not get out of bed, so he called out of work. Day 3, a heaviness set in his chest as he thought about the idea of going back into the office. At the point of "no call, no show," Everette was filled with so much sadness and didn't know what to do. He wanted to feel better. He was *waiting* to feel better. Overworked and overwhelmed, Everette did not realize how he arrived at that point.

SOUNDS LIKE DEPRESSION?

Depression can show up in different ways disguised as restlessness, irritability, anger, exhaustion with little things, withdrawal from activities, etc. The enemy wants you to think that there is no way around depression – the door is shut. This is the end of your story.

No! This too shall pass!

SHIFT YOUR FOCUS!

Let me remind you that the DEVIL IS A LIAR! **There *IS* a way out for you today!**

"I am the way and the truth and the life. *John 14:6 NIV*

JESUS IS THE ANSWER!

You can claim victory over depression knowing that Jesus loves you and is **always** there for you when you turn to Him!

As David reminds us:

> "The Lord is close to the brokenhearted and saves those who are crushed in spirit." *Psalms 34:18*

Isn't that good news? Jesus understands us in all our mental, physical, and emotional capacities. Remember, Jesus was fully human. He experienced similar emotions especially when he learned of His purpose to sacrifice for us all. In all of this, Jesus was **NEVER** alone. He turned to our Heavenly Father and to his disciples for comfort and support.

So, be encouraged today and don't give up hope. Remember, you are never alone with Jesus by your side.

Find a bit of "Joy" in your day. When was the last time you laughed out loud at something? Or allowed yourself to be silly just for a moment? What is something that brings a smile to your face?

TIME TO PRIORITIZE SELF-CARE

Self-care is a focus on the wellness needs in your life. Our mental, physical, spiritual, and emotional needs are all part of the wellness package.

Self-Care is *self-love* - remember that! God loves you and wants you to take care of yourself, and there are ways to do that in your life. Take heed to this important message today!

MORE REFLECTIONS:

1. Did you do something nice for yourself this week?
2. How often do you connect with friends/family?
3. Did you take a break at work today?
4. When was the last time you took a moment to relax?
5. Is it time to plan for a vacation?

Considering all of this, how can you fill your cup today?

Here are some examples:

Spiritual: Spend more time with God in prayer. Remind yourself of God's goodness by reading His word.

Physical: Take a walk outside and soak up some sun! Getting natural vitamin D from the sun is good for your emotional and mental wellness. (i.e., it can help improve mood) Plus, you can enhance your physical wellness by walking, so it's an all-around win!

Mental: Take a *real* break at work (no more working lunches!)

Emotional: if you feel overwhelmed at work, that may be a signal to rally team support. Perhaps you can schedule a meeting with your supervisor to shift some responsibilities to lighten the burden.

DEVELOP AN ACTION PLAN

Create a short list of things you want to do for yourself. It can be the littlest of things such as taking a long bath, or perhaps a weekend trip with friends. Now, schedule it and make it happen. Don't overthink this process. Be intentional and move!

YOU GOT THIS!

If you want to dive more into self-care, feel free to explore the following e-journal:

"The Journal of Love"

@ https://sowl.co/s/beyt8A

This digital guide will give you step-by-step strategies on addressing wellness.

<u>Brook</u>

A young woman, known as Brook, wanted a better life for herself. She was raised in a small, close-knit community, always having high hopes for her life.

A huge part of Brook's value system was loyalty – one that was instilled in her by her parents at a very young age. For Brook, that meant showing up and at times going above and beyond for all those she loved – family and friends alike. You could always count on Brook. She was so supportive.

Over the next year, Brook began to experience some challenges. Starting with her health, she noticed certain changes in her body that were debilitating at times which kept her out of work for days on end. Brook soon realized that she needed help. Having come from a close-knit community, she decided to talk to her neighbors and friends about her health challenges and the need for support. A few friends would call to check on Brook; some would even stop by from time to time.

As the weeks progressed, Brook became increasingly frustrated that everyone stopped calling and visiting. So, she decided to call her closest friend to update her on the health progress. During that call, Brook discovered that her friend no longer wanted to support her because it was so depressing to see her in such distress. Dismayed by her friend's response, Brook chose to stay silent moving forward. She felt alone and lost all at once.

EMOTIONAL ABANDONMENT?

Maybe the friend in the situation is setting a boundary since she is navigating her own mental health challenges?

No matter the rationale, Brook *perceived* her circumstance as one of abandonment. She felt alone and lost and didn't know what else to do at that point. She really needed someone to support her emotional needs through phone calls, visits to the home, etc.

SHIFT YOUR FOCUS

Here's the reality. People will change. Loved ones will disappoint you. Friends may leave you. Others may try to bring harm to you.

But Jesus will always be there for you. He will NEVER leave you or forsake you!

It is understandable to want support from friends and family in times such as these. But God is calling us to do something **bigger** in the waiting – turn to Him! While your phone may not always ring, know that God is waiting for you to answer *His* call. God has an open line for you! Remember His love, His goodness, and His grace. God's character is unchanging.

This immutability of God is what we ought to remember when we experience these things in life. No one can top that! Your friends, parents, children – no one, not even your spouse!

We can rely on Jesus to be our friend, our conqueror, our redeemer, our confident, our shield, our help, our shepherd. He doesn't change.

HE IS THE ONE IN WHOM WE RELY ON AND TRUST WITH EVERYTHING!

Thank you, Jesus!

"I the Lord do not change."

Malachi 3:6 NIV

Remember this declaration from God Himself. This is HUGE!

When you follow Jesus, He will be there for you!

Others turn their backs while *Jesus always has your back!*

When people are disloyal, *Jesus is always faithful and loyal!*

When you don't have help, **Jesus is your help!**

When you feel unloved – God *will surround you with His everlasting love.*

Your spouse may break a promise, but God *will follow through on all His promises!*

A friend may set a boundary of support to you, but God's *reach is boundless for you!*

When there is no one in your circle to count on, **you can** *always count on Jesus!*

Thank God for His unchanging hand!

<u>"The Kindness Pledge"</u>

- *I deserve kindness.*
- *God gives me grace, so I should apply self-compassion too.*
- *I can demonstrate kindness to others as a reflection of who I am in God.*
- *When kindness is not reciprocated, I can choose to be kind anyway.*
- *I am loved.*

@Renewtheview

FIND YOUR COMMUNITY

Sometimes, we create false narratives in our mind to soothe our ego or to predict the outcome of a situation. When we do so, we don't allow God to show up in our circumstances.

Let God be God.

The enemy will convince you that you don't belong to a community. That you don't deserve community. But God created us to be part of a community – not to do life alone. With God and the body of Christ, we have so much love and support in our lives. Remember that!

Here's a thought,

Create your "joy" list:

Reflect on some activities that you enjoy. It can be the littlest of things. Maybe it has been a while since you played tennis? Perhaps, you once enjoyed completing crossword puzzles in record time!

Write them down here. Feel free to expound on a separate sheet of paper.

1. ____________________________

2. ____________________________

3. ____________________________

4. ____________________________

5. ____________________________

Now, if you cannot recall or don't know where to start, it is not too late to begin anew!

Experience something new. Think about something that draws your interest, such as a hobby or activity. Maybe you previously wanted to try this but did not have the time or energy for it. What about now?

Are you ready? Is this *your* moment to make a change in your life for the better? If this is you, you are not alone. The key is to remember, that Jesus is right there with you through it all!

Intentionality is key. Schedule a day and time to do the activity of choice. Mark your calendars and set your alarms folks! Try this without thinking much about it and notice how you feel afterwards. It's not about when you feel like doing it; remember, you are trying to implement something new so just do it! You will soon discover more about yourself on this journey as you become more disciplined. Intentionality matters!

Remember, to give yourself grace in this process.

REFLECTION TIME:

What have you discovered about yourself over the last week or so?

<u>TAMMY</u>

Tammy serves as a volunteer at the food bank in her town. She firmly believes that doing deeds in the community is necessary and that is what motivates her each day. Throughout the week, community members donate to the food bank to help with the problem of food insecurity in that area. In fact, one day, Tammy was greeted by a young couple who had so much food to give that day! To the crew's surprise, it took several trips from their car to unload it all to the building! Tammy thanked the couple, but when they left, she expressed to other volunteers "this is too much food! Why did they bring so much at once? We are going to spend so much time organizing and stocking these items!"

Over the next few weeks, the donations started to decrease, leaving Tammy to declare: "We need more food. How are we going to have enough for the community? It's just not enough! Why can't we get a constant stream of donations from everyone? I just don't get it!"

The other volunteers shook their heads in dismay as Tammy slowly walked to the storage room.

COMPLAINING much?

Sometimes we can become frustrated when we don't get the results we were anticipating. In Tammy's case, she expected a steady flow of donations from the community. When her expectations were not met, she complained. When there was a previous overflow of donations, she complained.

In every circumstance, we ought to be thankful and humble ourselves as Jesus did for us.

God shows us an overflow in one season and a deficit in another, but He is still good. And even a "deficit" is a matter of perspective, right? Having a different flow at different moments in your life is still a reason to be thankful.

Complaining grieves the Holy Spirit.

How? Because God has demonstrated His goodness to you and has extended grace beyond measure, in so many ways. When you don't honor God with a heart of gratitude, you may miss the blessings ahead.

What will you do when the tides change in your life? How will you overcome some of the challenges presented to you?

-SHIFT YOUR FOCUS-

The reality is God will always provide when we put all our trust in Him. Perhaps if Tammy focused on gratitude, a different plan of action could have been executed. In other words, in the wait, consider dividing the food into smaller portions so that more can be shared amongst the community. Nothing is guaranteed; more donations, people showing up to help, etc. What is certain is God, Who is always faithful and always good and will always show up in due time. Now that is a fact of life!

> *"Trust in the Lord with all your heart and lean not on your own understanding;"*
> Proverbs 3:5 NIV

We will never fully understand how God works, but one thing is for sure He is a **God of love**, grace, faithfulness, joy, peace, understanding, justice, goodness, provision, patience, gentleness, wisdom, guidance and much more than we can utter!

We have our minds – focus on Him!
We have our hands - praise Him!
We have feet – serve in the community!
We have ears – listen and obey the word of God.
We have a voice – call on Him!
So, in the waiting room, we can move on our faith!

This is also a growth mindset. We need to understand that life is not just about us. We are called for something greater – to serve *His* purpose. His will be done!

When we face challenges, and uncertainties in life, *we must remember who we are in God.*

In the waiting room, understand that:

"you are the branches. If you remain in me and I in you, you will bear much fruit;" John 15:5 NIV

"You are the light of the world." Matthew 5:14 NIV

> "you are a chosen people, a royal priesthood, a holy nation, God's special possession, that you may declare the praises of him who called you out of darkness into his wonderful light."
>
> 1 Peter 2:9 NIV

What does it take for you to believe that you are *His child?* A child of the Most High! An heir to the kingdom! Heart break? Sickness? Loss? Depression?

Remember, you are *somebody* in Christ!

God is aware of your suffering, your circumstances and all, but don't you want to be free? You don't have to be held down or feel burdened by your situation. He will give us peace - he will give us rest. Trust in that today!

Gravitate towards what is right, what is good, what is holy. Gravitate towards God!

When you walk into the authority that God has given you, you won't fret in the waiting season. God is calling out to you in all circumstances! Embrace Him today!

Wait expectantly on the Lord, and you will soon discover how your life will transform for the better. The truth is God has always been there for you in the waiting room and will be there for you in the next season as well. The question is will you embrace Him? Will you be ready for Him?

Keep that hope in you always and know that at every moment, at each step, in this journey called life, you can be renewed in *Him!*

I would like to thank you for your support. Feel free to leave a review.

Peace and blessings to you!

Farrah-

For more tips and strategies, feel free to check out my other products and services:

An adult activity book for the believer of today!

Refocus on "joy" in your life.

AVAILABLE ON AMAZON!

Let's stay connected! I'm social too!

https://Renewtheview.co

DISCLAIMER:

To be clear, if you are experiencing mental/emotional health problems that significantly impair your daily functioning, please do not hesitate to seek a professional, such as a licensed therapist. While I have experience in this field, I am not a licensed therapist; I am a certified life coach.

My role is to encourage you and to offer practical tips and strategies that you can apply to your life. I hope to inspire you and motivate you to live a life full of Christ, and His love.

Farrah-

@Renewtheview

REFERENCES:

1. The Beck Institute (2020). *Understanding CBT.* The Beck Institute. Retrieved May 1, 2023, from https://beckinstitute.org/about/understanding-cbt/

2. *The Holy Bible.* (2011). Biblica, Inc. www.biblica.com (1973)

As the Founder of **Renew the View, LLC.**, Farrah Brown is delighted to offer mindset and wellness coaching to individuals today. Using her God-gifts, Farrah's mission is to encourage clients to challenge their mindset and shift their focus to reach their goals. She believes firmly that you can overcome things in life when you have the type of perspective that can lead you towards your breakthrough. Through her coaching services, books, and other products, Farrah is eager to motivate and inspire others to renew their view to become the best version of themselves today! https://Renewtheview.co

9 798218 338411